The Wild World of Animals

Foxes

Clever Hunters

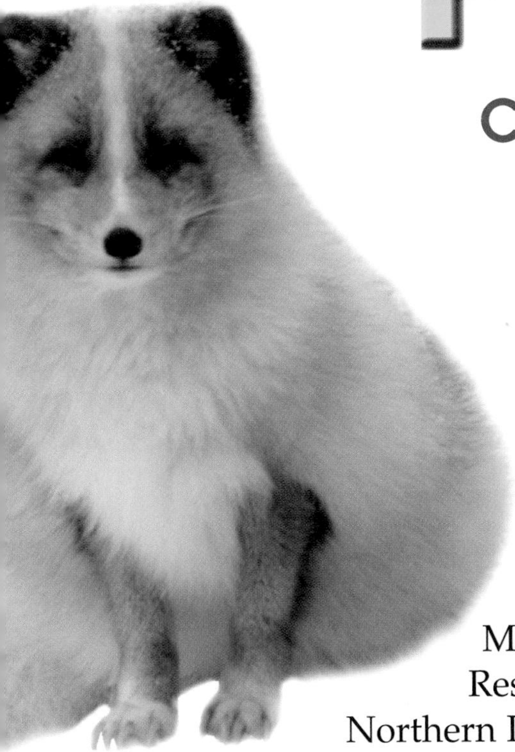

By Becky Olien

Consultant:
Marsha A. Sovada, Ph.D.
Research Wildlife Biologist
Northern Prairie Wildlife Research Center
U.S. Geological Survey

Bridgestone Books
an imprint of Capstone Press
Mankato, Minnesota

Bridgestone Books are published by Capstone Press
151 Good Counsel Drive, P.O. Box 669, Mankato, Minnesota 56002
http://www.capstone-press.com

Library of Congress Cataloging-in-Publication Data
Olien, Rebecca.
    Foxes: clever hunters/by Becky Olien.
    p. cm.—(The wild world of animals)
    Includes bibliographical references (p. 24) and index.
    Summary: A brief introduction to foxes, describing their physical characteristics, habitat,
young, food, predators, and relationship to people.
    ISBN 0-7368-1137-0
    1. Foxes—Juvenile literature. [1. Foxes.] I. Title. II. Series.
QL737.C22 O45 2002
599.775—dc21   2001004197

Editorial Credits
Erika Mikkelson, editor; Karen Risch, product planning editor; Linda Clavel, designer
    and illustrator; Heidi Schoof, photo researcher

Photo Credits
Digital Stock, 1
Eda Rogers, 8
Mary Ann McDonald, 6
PhotoDisc, Inc. (texture), 2, 3, 6, 8, 10, 12, 18, 22, 23, 24
Rick Hobbs, 4, 16
Robert McCaw, cover
Robin Brandt, 10
Thomas Kitchin/TOM STACK & ASSOCIATES, 12, 14, 18
Unicorn Stock Photos/Mark and Sue Werner, 20

1 2 3 4 5 6 07 06 05 04 03 02

Table of Contents

Foxes. 5

Foxes Are Mammals 7

A Fox's Habitat 9

What Do Foxes Eat? 11

Mating and Birth. 13

Fox Cubs 15

Predators 17

The Clever Fox 19

Foxes and People. 21

Hands On: A Fox's Sense of Smell. 22

Words to Know 23

Read More 24

Internet Sites 24

Index. 24

Foxes

Foxes can have red, white, gray, tan, or black fur. Foxes have strong jaws, sharp teeth, and long legs. Their muzzles are thin and pointed. Foxes have large, bushy tails.

muzzle
an animal's nose, mouth, and jaws

FUN FACTS

Arctic foxes have fur
that changes color. In
winter, their fur is white.
Their fur turns brown or
gray in summer.

arctic fox

Foxes Are Mammals

Foxes are mammals. They have a backbone. Foxes are warm-blooded. Female foxes feed milk to their young. Foxes belong to the dog family. Coyotes and wolves also are part of the dog family.

warm-blooded
having a body temperature that stays the same

fennec fox

FUN FACTS Fennec foxes live in North Africa, the Sinai Peninsula, and the Arabian Peninsula. These small foxes have hair on the bottoms of their paws. The hair protects them from the hot desert sand.

A Fox's Habitat

Foxes live in many habitats around the world. Arctic foxes make their homes in the frozen, treeless tundra. Fennec foxes live in deserts. Some gray foxes live in wooded areas. Gray foxes climb trees. Other fox habitats are fields and cities.

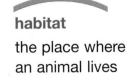

habitat
the place where
an animal lives

Foxes often catch more than they can eat. They bury their food for later. The buried food is called a cache (KASH).

red fox

What Do Foxes Eat?

Foxes are omnivores. They eat animals and plants. They eat squirrels, mice, lizards, and birds. Foxes also eat berries, fruits, and nuts.

omnivore

an animal that eats plants and animals

arctic foxes

Mating and Birth

A female fox is called a vixen. A male fox is called a dog fox. Vixens and dog foxes mate in the winter. In early spring, two to eight cubs are born in a den. A den can be a hollow log, cave, or hole in the ground.

hollow

having empty space inside of it

red foxes

Fox Cubs

Young foxes are called cubs, kits, or pups. Cubs cannot see at first. Vixens stay near their newborn cubs for two weeks. Dog foxes bring food to the vixen and the cubs. Fox cubs leave their parents when they are three months old.

red fox and coyote

Predators

Foxes have many predators. Coyotes, lynx, cougars, and wolves hunt foxes for food. Many foxes are hit by cars and killed. Farmers kill foxes that eat their chickens. Some people kill foxes for sport. In England, fox hunts are popular events.

FUN FACTS !

Gray foxes are the only members of the dog family to climb trees. They jump from branch to branch. They sometimes climb a tree to take a nap.

gray fox

The Clever Fox

Foxes are difficult for people and predators to catch. Foxes learn to stay away from danger. They use their good senses of smell and hearing to escape being trapped. Foxes also can live in many different places. They can find food almost anywhere.

red fox

Foxes and People

Some people do not like foxes. Foxes eat chickens and other small animals. But foxes also help farmers. They eat mice and other rodents. People sometimes take over foxes' habitats. The foxes then leave for new areas. Some foxes can learn to live in cities.

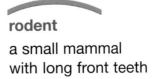

rodent
a small mammal
with long front teeth

Hands On: A Fox's Sense of Smell

Foxes can smell through several inches (centimeters) of snow. You can compare your sense of smell to a fox's sense of smell.

What You Need

Large paper cup
Ruler
Pencil
Ground cinnamon
Whipped topping

What You Do

1. Place the ruler along the outside of the cup. Mark inches or centimeters from the bottom to the top of the cup.
2. Sprinkle just enough cinnamon into the cup to cover the bottom. Place your nose above the cup and smell.
3. Spoon 1 inch (2.5 centimeters) of whipped topping into the cup. Sniff the cup again. Can you still smell the cinnamon?
4. If you can smell the cinnamon, spoon another inch or centimeter of whipped topping into the cup. Sniff again.
5. Repeat as many times as you need to until you can no longer smell cinnamon.

How many inches or centimeters of whipped topping could you smell through? Most people can smell through only 1 or 2 inches (2.5 or 5 centimeters) of whipped topping. A fox can smell a mouse that is under 5 inches (13 centimeters) of snow.

Words to Know

cache (KASH)—a place where an animal hides its food

mammal (MAM-uhl)—a warm-blooded animal with a backbone; mammals feed milk to their young.

mate (MATE)—to join together to produce young

peninsula (puh-NIN-suh-luh)—an area of land surrounded by water on three sides; some fennec foxes live on the Sinai Peninsula and the Arabian Peninsula.

predator (PRED-uh-tur)—an animal that hunts other animals for food

tundra (TUHN-dra)—a treeless area of frozen soil in the far north

Read More

Greenaway, Theresa. *Wolves, Wild Dogs, and Foxes.* The Secret World Of. Austin, Texas: Raintree Steck-Vaughn, 2001.

Lantier, Patricia, and Judy Schuler. *The Wonder of Foxes.* Animal Wonders. Milwaukee: Gareth Stevens, 2001.

Internet Sites

Canadian Wildlife Service—Hinterland Who's Who—Red Fox
http://www.cws-scf.ec.gc.ca/hww-fap/redfox/redfox.html

Foxes Online
http://www.foxes-online.com

The Red Fox
http://www.foxbox.org/fact/factsheet/index.html

Index

coyotes, 7, 17
cubs, 13, 15
den, 13
deserts, 9
farmers, 17, 21
fur, 5
habitats, 9, 21
jaws, 5
legs, 5

mammals, 7
muzzles, 5
omnivores, 11
predators, 17, 19
rodents, 21
tails, 5
tundra, 9
vixen, 13, 15
wolves, 7, 17